DESSERT DESIGNER

CREATIONS YOU CAN MAKE and Eat!

by Dana Meachen Rau

capstone

Published by Capstone Young Readers,
1710 Roe Crest Drive, North Mankato, Minnesota 56003.
www.capstoneyoungreaders.com

Library of Congress Cataloging-in-Publication Data
Rau, Dana Meachen, 1971–
Dessert Designer: creations you can make and eat / by Dana
Meachen Rau.
   pages cm.—(Capstone young readers.)
Audience: Ages 10-10
Audience: Grades 4 to 6.
   Summary: "Step-by-step instructions teach readers how to create
food art with cakes, cupcakes, cookies, and candies"— Provided by
publisher.
   ISBN 978-1-62370-006-5 (pbk.)
1. Cake decorating—Juvenile literature. 2. Cake—Juvenile
literature. I. Title.
TX771.2.R378 2013
641.86'539—dc23   2012025571

Editor: Jennifer Besel
Designer: Juliette Peters
Food and Photo Stylist: Brent Bentrott
Prop Preparation: Sarah Schuette
Scheduler: Marcy Morin

Photo Credits:
All photos by Capstone Studio/Karon Dubke

Printed in China.
092012
006936RRDS13

Table of Contents

Introduction

Cupcakes

PLAY WITH YOUR FOOD!

Your kitchen is more than a place to make supper. It's an art studio. When you combine dessert and your imagination, you can create amazing works of art that taste as good as they look! Turn cakes into roller coasters. Top cupcakes with crazy creatures. Make cookies hoot with awesomeness and candy flutter your taste buds. There's no end to what you can do with desserts!

How to Use This Book

Ready to get started? It's a piece of cake! Start by gathering the supplies you need. You may already have the ingredients in your kitchen. But if not, all the supplies can be found in grocery stores, convenience stores, or the cake-decorating aisles of craft and hobby stores.

~ Use Your Imagination ~
The ideas in this book are just that—ideas! Don't like a color or decoration we used? Change it! Can't find the same candy? Use something else. The best part of dessert designing is getting to be creative. Have fun!

~ The Best Part! ~

Some might argue that frosting is the most important part of a dessert. Stores sell super-tasty tubs of premade frosting. But if you want to whip up your own, here's a simple recipe. It makes about 2½ cups (600 milliliters) of frosting.

Ingredients
½ cup (120 mL) unsalted butter, softened to room temperature
½ teaspoon (2.5 mL) vanilla extract
2 cups (480 mL) confectioners' sugar
1–2 tablespoons (15–30 mL) milk

Tools
large bowl
measuring cups and spoons
electric hand mixer
spatula

Steps
1. In a large bowl, cream the butter and vanilla with the mixer on medium speed until fluffy.
2. Beating on low, alternate adding sugar and milk until the ingredients are mixed well. The frosting should be thick, creamy, and spreadable. Scrape the sides of the bowl often with the spatula.
3. Store the frosting in the refrigerator in an airtight container. Bring it to room temperature and rewhip before using.

For chocolate frosting, follow the recipe above, and add ¼ cup (60 mL) unsweetened cocoa powder along with the sugar.

ROYAL ICING

For many recipes in this book, you'll need to make royal icing. Royal icing hardens into a firm shell so your dessert has a smooth finish. There are two kinds of royal icing. Flood royal icing is thinner and good for filling in large areas. Edge icing is thicker and good for making details and edges.

Edge Icing

2 teaspoons (10 mL) meringue powder
2 tablespoons (30 mL) water
2 to 2½ cups (480 to 600 mL) confectioners' sugar

With a mixer on high, blend the ingredients together in a bowl for about four to five minutes. The icing is the right consistency when it forms little peaks that hold their shape.

Makes 1 cup (240 mL) of icing

Flood Icing

Make a batch of edge icing. Then add water ½ teaspoon (2.5 mL) at a time, blending after each addition. The icing is ready when drips hold their shape for just a moment before they blend back into the icing.

Keep royal icing in an airtight container when you're not using it. If you don't, a crust will start to form on the top. You can keep icing for about a week at room temperature. Rewhip before you use it.

DECORATOR'S TOOLBOX

A painter needs brushes and canvases. A carpenter needs hammers and nails. A dessert designer like you needs tools too!

~ parchment paper ~
Use this paper to line cookie sheets that will go in the oven. Unlike wax paper, parchment paper won't smoke if it gets hot.

~ toothpicks and wooden skewers ~
These are great for helping keep layers together or to stick decorations to a project.

~ cookie cutters ~
These are great for forming cookie dough into shapes. But you can also use them to cut already baked round sugar cookies into shapes too!

~ decorating tips ~
These go on the piping bag to create cool designs with frosting.

~ cookie sheet ~
This works as well in the refrigerator as it does in the oven to keep treats from rolling around.

~ rolling pin ~
This is a handy tool for flattening taffies or crushing candies.

~ kitchen shears ~
These scissors are designed for use with food.

~ lollipop sticks ~
You'll be surprised what amazing things you can stick to the ends of these!

~fondue fork ~
This tiny fork is great for dipping small pieces of cake into frosting.

~ piping bag ~
This fabric or plastic bag holds frosting and is used to decorate desserts.

~ turntable ~
This spinning tool makes it easy to frost all sides of a cake without accidently putting your elbow in it!

~ sharp knife ~
You need this to cut or score candy and baked goods.

~ cooling rack ~
Not only is this tool great for cooling goodies, but the slats let frosting drip off a project for a smooth finish.

~ wax paper ~
Use this supply to keep taffy and other sticky stuff from sticking to your workspace.

~ bowls ~
Keep a variety of these around to mix up frosting. Make sure that bowls used for melting candy are microwave safe.

~ aluminum foil ~
Sure, foil keeps foods from sticking. But it also looks great as wrapping for lollipops!

~ spreader ~
This might be the most handy decorating tool. Use it to cover a surface with a smooth layer of frosting.

~ iron ~
It's surprising, but an iron can be a handy kitchen tool. Use it to melt licorice pieces together.

~ tweezers ~
Use tweezers to place those tiny decorations in just the right place.

~ twisty ties ~
Use these handy wires to tie up goody bags.

~ cutting board ~
Do any cutting on the cutting board to avoid damaging kitchen counters.

~ fork ~
This isn't just for eating with! Use a fork to pick up cupcakes to make them easier to frost.

~ zip-top bags ~
These make a great substitute for piping bags.

~ food coloring ~
Food coloring makes your frosting and icing stand out. Just put a drop of liquid or a dab of gel into your frosting. You'll find a little goes a long way.

~ hammer ~
This tool isn't just for the wood shop! Use a hammer to crush hard candies into meltable pieces.

~ spoons ~
Have a bunch of spoons ready to stir up frosting or icing in a rainbow of colors.

ALOHA LEI CUPCAKES

A Hawaiian luau is the ultimate beach bash. Tropical parties need necklaces of flowers—especially ones you can eat! Enjoy these tasty blooms, then hula until sunset.

INGREDIENTS
vanilla frosting
12 mini cupcakes
36 jellybeans
96 wafer candies
   in a variety of colors
18 green wafer candies

1. Frost the top of each cupcake.

2. Place three jellybeans in the center of each cupcake. Surround the jellybeans with four wafer candy petals. Then add four more petals behind the first ones.

3. With an adult's help, gently drag a knife across the surfaces of the green wafers to score them. Don't try to cut straight through the wafers or they will crack.

4. Break the green wafers in half along the scored line.

5. Tuck the green wafer pieces behind the petals to look like leaves.

6. Arrange the cupcakes on a platter to look like a lei.

~ A BASKET OF BLOOMS ~
You can also arrange these flower cupcakes in a basket. Cut a block of flower foam to fit tightly in a basket. Cover the foam with plastic wrap. Poke a lollipop stick into the foam. Place a cupcake on the stick to hold it in place. Repeat with more lollipop sticks and cupcakes until you have a bunch of beautiful blooms.

BERRY BASKET

A tisket, a tasket, a tasty cupcake basket. Serve up these cupcakes for a *berry* amazing treat!

INGREDIENTS
vanilla frosting
1 mini cupcake
    (paper liner removed)
1 graham cracker square
8 vanilla or chocolate cream
    wafer cookies
1 orange or brown licorice twist
raspberries, blackberries,
    or blueberries

1. Frost the top of the cupcake. Also spread some frosting on the bottom of the cupcake. Set the cupcake on the graham cracker to make a base.

2. Spread frosting on one wide side of each wafer cookie. Stack the cookies around the cupcake like a basket. If needed, add frosting to the edges to help them stick to the cupcake and base.

3. Arch the licorice twist and tuck it into opposite corners of the basket.

4. Place the berries on top of the cupcake so it looks like a full basket.

5. For a special touch, add a ribbon to the handle.

~ SWEETS IN ALL SEASONS ~
When berries are out of season, look for raspberry and blackberry candies. They'll give you a taste of summer any time of year!

FLUFFY BUNNY

Turn a cupcake into a hopping good treat.
This sweet little bunny is so fluffy and cute,
you'll just eat it up.

INGREDIENTS

1 cupcake (paper liner removed)
vanilla frosting
sweetened flake coconut
1 large, thin, round
    chocolate cookie
1 jumbo marshmallow
pink decorating sugar
1 large marshmallow
2 mini marshmallows
2 small breath mints
1 pink jellybean
2 chocolate pastels

Tip:
Frosting spreads best when it's kept at room temperature. But cupcakes at room temperature can be soft and fragile. Place cooled cupcakes in a zip-top bag. Then put them in the freezer for about an hour. Freezing makes them firmer, which makes them easier to frost.

1. Stick a fork into the top of the cupcake. Holding the fork in one hand, frost the top, bottom, and sides of the cupcake.

2. Sprinkle coconut over the cupcake until the frosting is completely covered. Remove the fork, and place the cupcake upside down on the chocolate cookie.

3. Hold the jumbo marshmallow so the long sides are up and down. Cut skinny slices off the right and left sides to make bunny ears. One side of each ear will be sticky. Poke toothpicks into the bottoms of the ears. Sprinkle the sticky sides with pink decorating sugar. Poke the ears into the top of the cupcake.

4. Cut the large marshmallow in half. Place the halves at the base of the cupcake as feet.

5. Use a dab of frosting to stick a mini marshmallow in the back as a tail.

6. Cut a mini marshmallow in half. Stick the halves to the face as cheeks. Using frosting as glue, add the mints as teeth and the jellybean as a nose. Finally, add two chocolate pastels as eyes.

GIFTS FROM the SEA

A day at the beach is full of splashes, sand, and sun. Discover what the waves washed in with this cupcake covered with ocean treasures.

INGREDIENTS
vanilla frosting
1 cupcake
blue food coloring
1 graham cracker
1 piece each of purple, orange, red, and green taffy
1 sugar pearl
1 red round fruit candy

~ Piping Tips ~
Experiment with different piping tips to get the look you want when decorating with frosting. Round tips are great for outlining details. Basket weave tips can make long, ribbed stripes.

Tip:
Squeeze the taffy between your fingers and in your hands. The warmth of your skin will soften the taffy and make it easy to work with.

1. Frost the cupcake with vanilla frosting. Then mix up blue frosting. Pipe the blue frosting over half of the white frosting, making swirls like waves.

2. With a rolling pin, crush the graham cracker into crumbs. Sprinkle the crumbs on the white half of the cupcake.

3. To make the oyster shell, flatten purple taffy between two sheets of wax paper. With the kitchen shears, cut the taffy into a heart shape. Fold the heart in half to make a shell shape and pinch the pointy end closed. Place a sugar pearl inside the shell.

4. To make the starfish, flatten orange taffy. Cut the orange taffy into a star shape. Mold the cut edges smooth with your fingers.

5. To make the crab, flatten red taffy into a circle. Place the red fruit candy under the center of the circle and press the taffy to it. Snip claw and leg shapes into the taffy around the fruit candy.

6. To make the seaweed, flatten green taffy. Cut grass shapes.

7. Place your ocean treasures on top of the sand side of the cupcake.

movie POPCORN TREAT

You can't watch a movie without popcorn. But you also need a treat to satisfy your sweet tooth. No problem! Create the ultimate movie snack with this cupcake covered in candy popcorn.

INGREDIENTS
yellow food coloring
vanilla frosting
1 cupcake
5 white candy melting wafers
crushed ice
water

1. Mix up a batch of pale yellow frosting. Frost the top of the cupcake.

2. To make the candy popcorn, place the melting wafers in a small zip-top bag or disposable piping bag. Leave the bag open and microwave on the defrost setting for 30 seconds. Squeeze the melted candy to one corner. If the wafers are not soft yet, microwave on defrost 30 seconds more. With a kitchen shears, snip off the corner of the bag.

3. Fill a shallow bowl with crushed ice and water. Squeeze dollops of the melted candy into the ice water. They will cool almost instantly into popcorn shapes.

4. Remove the candy popcorn from the water and dry on a paper towel. Then place the popcorn on top of the cupcake.

5. For the movie theater look, cut about 3 inches (7.6 centimeters) off the top of a popcorn bag. Open it up, and place the small bag around your cupcake.

Tip:
Melting wafers are solid candy circles that can be melted easily. The melted candy can be used for dipping or molding into new shapes. Each package has directions, so be sure to follow them carefully.

GRINNING GORILLA

It can be a jungle out there. This grinning gorilla will give you a sweet burst of happiness to brighten any day.

INGREDIENTS
chocolate frosting
1 chocolate cupcake
chocolate sprinkles
1 large thin chocolate cookie
2 chocolate-covered cookies
1 chocolate-covered pretzel
2 mini creme-filled
　　chocolate cookies
2 brown candy-coated chocolates

1. Frost the cupcake with chocolate frosting. Then cover the frosting with chocolate sprinkles.

2. Place the large, thin cookie in the center of the cupcake.

3. Spread a bit of frosting on the bottoms of the chocolate covered cookies. Stack them on top of the thin cookie to look like a gorilla's face. Top the stack with a pretzel to make the snout.

4. Open the mini chocolate cookies. Use the creme-filled sides for the eyes. Put a dab of frosting on the backs to serve as glue. Then frost on the candy-coated chocolates for eyeballs.

5. On each side of the face, add the other halves of the creme-filled cookies as ears.

~ DID YOU KNOW? ~
Cupcake pans (also known as muffin tins) were called gem pans in the early 1900s.

PEACEFUL snowman

You may like snowball fights, but the snowmen sure don't! Show the snowman's point of view with this hilarious creation.

INGREDIENTS
vanilla frosting
1 cupcake
white sparkling sugar
1 large marshmallow
5 chocolate melting wafers
1 wafer candy
2 chocolate pastels
1 piece orange taffy
1 red licorice whip
2 starlight mints

Tip:
You can buy piping bags and tips at cake decorating and craft stores. Or you can make your own using a zip-top plastic bag. Scoop frosting into the bag, squeeze out the extra air, and seal it closed. Then squeeze the frosting to one corner. With a scissors, snip a hole in the corner. Cut a small hole for detailed decorations or a wide one to cover large areas.

1. Frost the cupcake with a "cupcake swirl" by piping a circle around the edge. Continue in a spiral shape into the center. Lift the bag at the end to give your frosting a little peak.

2. Sprinkle the frosting with white sparkling sugar.

3. Place the marshmallow on a fork. Holding the fork in one hand, frost the marshmallow until it's covered completely. Then sprinkle the marshmallow with sparkling sugar. Gently take it off the fork and place it on the cupcake.

4. Place the melting wafers in a small zip-top bag. Leave the bag open and microwave on the defrost setting for 30 seconds. Squeeze the melted candy to one corner. If the wafers are not soft yet, microwave on defrost 30 seconds more. With a kitchen shears, snip off the corner of the bag.

5. On a piece of wax paper, pipe the melted chocolate into shapes that look like stick arms. Pipe a peace sign on the wafer candy. Let them dry for at least one hour. Then put them on your snowman.

6. Add two chocolate pastels for eyes. Roll a bit of orange taffy into a nose, and stick it on the marshmallow.

7. To make earmuffs, cut a small length of licorice whip and arch it over the top of the marshmallow. Glue one starlight mint on each side with a dab of frosting.

sweet TWEET

Explore nature's surprises with this fun dessert. Everyone will be tweeting your praises!

INGREDIENTS
1 cup (240 mL)
    butterscotch chips
½ cup (120 mL) chow
    mein noodles
green food coloring
vanilla frosting
1 cupcake
1 piece each of green
    and orange taffy
1 mini white marshmallow
blue sparkling sugar
3 blue jellybeans

1. Heat the butterscotch chips in the microwave for 30 seconds. Stir. Continue melting at 15-second intervals until all the chips are melted.

2. Stir in the chow mein noodles until well coated with butterscotch.

3. Line a cookie sheet with wax paper. Drop large spoonfuls of the noodle mixture onto the cookie sheet. With the back of the spoon, press a bowl into the middle of each one.

4. Place the nests in the refrigerator for about 15 to 20 minutes.

5. Mix up a batch of green frosting. Pipe leaves of frosting around the edge of the cupcake.

6. Place a nest on the cupcake.

7. Roll a tiny piece of green taffy to look like an inchworm. Place it on the nest.

8. Flatten the orange taffy and cut out a small diamond. Fold the diamond in half to make a beak. Stick the beak to the mini marshmallow with frosting.

9. Brush the marshmallow just above the beak with a bit of water to make it sticky. Use tweezers to place two pieces of blue sparkling sugar on as eyes.

10. Place your chick in the nest. Surround it with three jellybeans to look like unhatched eggs.

TIPSY FLOWER TOWER

Celebrate your un-birthday with this tipsy cake. It's so beautifully strange, you'll feel like you stepped into Wonderland.

INGREDIENTS

2 cupcakes
  (paper liners removed)
1 mini cupcake
  (paper liner removed)
vanilla frosting
pink, purple, and green
  food coloring
sugar pearls
2 pieces pink taffy

1. Freeze your cupcakes for about an hour. Then cut the tops off the two large cupcakes on a slant.

2. Spread some frosting on the bottom of one cupcake. Place it on top of the other one. Arrange so that the slanted tops are opposite each other.

3. Spread frosting on the bottom of the mini cupcake, and stick it on top.

4. Push a wooden skewer down through the center of all three layers to hold them together. Then return the cupcakes to the freezer for another 15 to 30 minutes or until firm again.

5. Meanwhile, mix up a batch of pink frosting in a microwave safe bowl. Heat for about 15 seconds in the microwave. Stir. You want the frosting to be a liquid, pourable consistency. Heat another 15 seconds if it is still too thick.

6. Place the cupcake tower on a cooling rack with wax paper below. Spoon the melted frosting over all the cupcakes until they are well coated. When the excess frosting has all dripped off, transfer the tower to a plate. Put it in the refrigerator for 10 to 15 minutes.

7. Mix up a batch of purple frosting. Pipe stripes on the middle cake. With the stripes still wet, place a sugar pearl at the top of each stripe.

8. Mix up a batch of green frosting. Pipe leaf designs on the top and bottom cakes. Add sugar pearls as accents.

9. Flatten one piece of taffy with a rolling pin. Cut it into about five small flower petal shapes. Roll one petal into a tube, and pinch one end closed. Attach the other petals to the pinched end and flair them out to make a rose. Repeat with the second piece of taffy.

10. Attach the roses on the tower with a dab of frosting.

GLITZY ARMADILLO

Scaly armadillos get no respect. But this one is ready for the spotlight. Your friends will want a photo of this treat topper ... before they gobble it up!

INGREDIENTS
1 cupcake
chocolate frosting
2 peanut butter sandwich cookies
purple food coloring
vanilla frosting
purple decorating sugar
2 orange circus peanuts

Tip:
If pieces fall off, try sticking toothpicks into the cookie and circus peanut pieces. Then stick the toothpicks in the cupcake.

1. Frost the cupcake with chocolate frosting.

2. Cut both cookies in half. Then on two of the halves, trim off a little more so they are shorter than the other two.

3. Mix up a batch of purple frosting. Pipe a purple edge around each cookie. Then sprinkle the purple frosting with the decorating sugar.

4. Place the two taller cookie pieces in the center of the cupcake. Place the shorter pieces in front of and behind the other two cookies.

5. Cut one of the circus peanuts in half. Mold one half of the candy into a head shape. Snip into the two corners on the top to make two triangles. Fold them up to look like ears. Attach the head in front of the cookies.

6. Pipe two dabs of chocolate frosting on the head for eyes.

7. Cut slices from the other half of the circus peanut to make four legs. Attach two on each side of the cookies.

8. Cut a crescent shape from the second circus peanut for a tail. Attach it behind the cookies.

9. Pipe vanilla frosting on the tips of each leg for claws.

SUGAR BURGER

There's no meat or veggies in this burger. It's just two cupcake buns filled with frosting and candy. Add a side of candy cheese curls, and dessert becomes a meal.

INGREDIENTS
2 yellow cake cupcakes
   (paper liners removed)
chocolate frosting
green and red fruit leather
1 red fruit slice
yellow food coloring
vanilla frosting
1 green gumdrop
2 orange circus peanuts

Tip:
Don't worry too much about how this cupcake looks from the top. It's more important to think about its view from the side. Keep your candies close enough to the edge so they'll be seen when you put on the top bun.

1. Cut the tops off of the cupcakes. Place one top down on a plate.

2. Pipe the chocolate frosting in a circle around the edge. Continue piping in a spiral shape to fill the bottom "bun."

3. For lettuce, cut green fruit leather into thin strips. Place around the edges of the frosting.

4. For tomatoes, cut the red fruit slice into slices. Place on top of the lettuce.

5. Mix up a small batch of yellow frosting. Pipe the frosting over the candy to look like mustard.

6. Spread vanilla frosting on the bottom of the other cupcake bun to look like mayonnaise. Place this bun on top of the stack.

7. For the olive, cut a small hole into the top of the gumdrop. Roll up a small bit of red fruit leather, and stick that in the gumdrop's hole. Poke a toothpick through the gumdrop, and then stick the toothpick into the top of your cupcake.

8. For the cheese curls, cut the circus peanuts in half. Mold each strip into a crescent shape.

hoT COCOA CUP

What's better than a cup of cocoa on a cold winter day? Cupcakes, of course! Combine the two, and you have the best way to top off a snowy day.

INGREDIENTS
2 chocolate cupcakes (paper
    liners removed)
chocolate frosting
1 peppermint stick
5 green candy melting wafers
green food coloring
vanilla frosting
3 mini marshmallows

1. Stack the cupcakes, gluing the bottom of one cupcake to the top of the other with some chocolate frosting. Trim the edges so that they form a smooth mug shape from top to bottom.

2. Push the peppermint stick into the cupcakes from the top at an angle. This stick will help hold the cakes together.

3. Frost the top of the cupcake with chocolate frosting. Make swirls to look like hot cocoa.

4. Place the melting wafers in a small zip-top bag. Leave the bag open. Microwave on the defrost setting for 30 seconds. Squeeze the melted candy to one corner. If the wafers are not soft yet, microwave on defrost 30 seconds more. With a kitchen shears, snip off the corner of the bag.

5. On a piece of wax paper, pipe the melted wafers into a "C" shape. Let it harden for about 30 minutes.

6. Mix up a batch of green frosting to match the color of your melting wafers. Frost the sides of the cupcakes. Pipe a clean edge of green frosting around the top.

7. Stick the dried melting wafer "C" on the side of your mug as the handle.

8. Decorate the top of the cupcake with mini marshmallows.

LOTS OF LAVA

Create this cupcake flowing with frosting lava, and your family will erupt in applause.

INGREDIENTS
1 chocolate cupcake
  (paper liner removed)
1 large marshmallow
chocolate frosting
red food coloring
vanilla frosting
2 red hard candies

1. Turn the cupcake upside-down. Glue the marshmallow to the cupcake bottom with a dollop of frosting.

2. Pipe chocolate frosting in circles around the marshmallow and cupcake so it looks like a mini mountain.

3. Mix up a batch of red frosting. Pipe it on the top and sides to look like flowing lava.

4. Unwrap the hard candies, and place them in a sturdy zip-top bag. With a rolling pin, crush the candy into powdery bits.

5. Preheat your oven to 350 degrees Fahrenheit (177 degrees Celsius). Line a cookie sheet with parchment paper.

6. Pour the candy bits onto the cookie sheet. Gently shake the tray so the crushed candies make a flat layer. Make sure you can't see the parchment paper between any of the candy bits.

7. Bake the candy for two minutes or until it melts. Using oven mitts, remove the tray from the oven and let cool at least 30 minutes.

8. Break the candy into pieces, and stick them into the top of your volcano to look like shooting lava.

CLEAR SKY RAINBOWS

After a thunderstorm the skies clear, and nature treats you to an amazing colorful display. Bring a rainbow into the kitchen with a 3-D display of your own.

INGREDIENTS
edge royal icing
red, orange, yellow, green, blue, and purple food coloring
2 large round sugar cookies
flood royal icing
1 chocolate covered caramel
10 pieces yellow candy buttons

1. Divide the edge icing into eight bowls. Keep one bowl white. Tint six of the bowls into the colors of the rainbow. Tint the last bowl a light blue. Place the icings into eight piping bags.

2. Cut one cookie in half. On one half, use white icing to pipe half a cloud shape in the right-hand corner. With the red icing, pipe an arch along the outer edge of the cookie to meet the cloud. Repeat with the orange, yellow, green, blue, and purple.

3. Divide the flood icing into two bowls. Keep one bowl white. Tint the other light blue.

4. Spoon white flood icing into the cloud shape. Then spoon blue flood icing into the small arch under your rainbow. Use a toothpick to spread the icing. Set the cookie aside for about 30 minutes until the icing hardens.

5. Next, pipe a ring of light blue edge icing around the outer edge of the full cookie. Pipe a cloud shape on the right side with the white edge icing. Spoon white flood icing into the cloud shape and blue flood icing onto the rest of the cookie.

6. While the flood icing is still wet, place the rainbow upright on top. Match up the clouds on both cookies.

7. Cover the bottom of a chocolate covered caramel with yellow edge icing. Stick the candy buttons to the icing to look like gold coins. Place your pot of gold at the end of the rainbow.

8. Let the cookie sit for a few hours to completely harden.

WISE OLD OWL

You're one smart cookie. So are owls. These
wise birds won't help you with your homework.
But they know a lot about being delicious!

INGREDIENTS

edge royal icing
purple, blue, and brown
    food coloring
1 large round sugar cookie
flood royal icing
2 white candy wafers
1 orange jelly bean
yellow fruit leather

1. Divide the edge icing into three
small bowls. Add purple food coloring
to one, blue to another, and leave the
third white.

2. With the purple edge icing, pipe a
half-circle shape onto the top half of the
cookie. Pipe triangles down each side.

3. With the blue icing, complete the
circle by piping a line to connect
the bottoms of the two triangles.

4. Mix up a batch of flood icing. Divide it
into two bowls. Add purple to one bowl
and blue to the other to match the edge
icing colors.

5. Spoon the purple flood icing into the
purple triangles and half circle. Spoon
the blue flood icing into the middle area.
Spread the icings with toothpicks to fill in
the areas completely.

6. Pipe horizontal lines with the white
edge icing across the blue area. With a
toothpick, drag lines through the blue icing
from bottom to top, and then back down
again. This will make white feather shapes.

7. Place the wafer candies and orange jelly
bean onto the cookie to make the owl's face.
Color a bit of white edge icing brown. Pipe
two brown icing dots for eyes.

8. Cut a small triangle from the fruit
leather. Snip one edge to look like feathers.
Round the corner opposite the feather
snips, and carefully fit the leather between
the eyes.

9. Let the cookie sit for a few hours to
completely harden.

> *Tip:*
> Dragging a toothpick through lines of
> icing can create some cool effects, such
> as feathers, tie-dye, or fireworks.

FANCY TOPPER

Ready to create a red carpet showstopper that's good enough to eat? Hats off to this glamorous project.

INGREDIENTS
chocolate melting wafers
pink food coloring
edge royal icing
flood royal icing
1 large round sugar cookie
1 vanilla sandwich cookie
buttercream frosting

1. Place five melting wafers in a small zip-top bag. Leave the bag open and microwave on the defrost setting for 30 seconds. Squeeze the melted candy to one corner. If the wafers are not soft yet, microwave on defrost 30 seconds more. With a kitchen shears, snip off the corner of the bag.

2. On a piece of wax paper, pipe the melted chocolate into shapes that will decorate your hat. Let them dry for at least one hour.

3. Mix up batches of pink edge and flood icings. Pipe a blob of edge icing into the middle of the large cookie. Place the sandwich cookie on top.

4. Pipe a ring of edge icing around the outer edge of the bottom cookie.

5. Spoon the flood icing on top of the sandwich cookie. It will pour over the sides and down onto the bottom cookie. Spread with a toothpick to cover all areas.

6. While the icing is wet, place your chocolate decorations against the top cookie.

7. Let the cookie hat sit for a few hours to completely harden.

8. Pipe more melted chocolate around the bottom of the small cookie. If you wish, use buttercream frosting to add frosting flowers or other decorations to the hat.

PUDDLE WITCH

When the wicked witch melted, who knew she would leave so much sweetness behind?

INGREDIENTS
green food coloring
edge royal icing
1 large round sugar cookie
flood royal icing
1 flat, round chocolate cookie
1 mini peanut butter cup
chocolate frosting
1 chocolate kiss
1 piece yellow taffy
1 pretzel stick
1 chocolate chew

~ Shaping Taffy ~
You can soften taffy by warming it in the microwave for about five seconds. Once the taffy is warm, flatten, roll, cut, or mold it into any shape you want. Be sure to cover your work surface with wax paper so the taffy won't stick.

1. Add green food coloring to the edge icing.

2. Pipe a ring of green edge icing around the cookie. Make it wavy like a puddle.

3. Tint the flood icing green to match your edge icing. Spoon the flood icing onto the cookie and spread with a toothpick to cover all areas.

4. For the hat, place the chocolate cookie on top of the green puddle. Glue the peanut butter cup to the flat cookie with a small blob of chocolate frosting. Use a dab of chocolate frosting to stick the kiss to the peanut butter cup.

5. For the broom, place the taffy between two pieces of wax paper. Roll it flat with a rolling pin. Then cut it into thin strips. Mold these strips onto one end of the pretzel stick. Pinch and roll a small piece of chocolate chew into a thin strip. Wrap the strip around the taffy and pretzel. Trim the ends of the yellow strips to the same length. Place the broom on the green puddle.

6. Let the cookie sit for a few hours to completely harden.

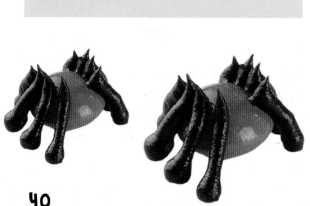

Want another idea to go with this witch?
Add a little spider that sits down beside her!

INGREDIENTS
edge royal icing
black food coloring
orange or purple round fruit candy

Mix up a batch of black edge icing. Place the fruit candy on a piece
of wax paper. Pipe eight icing legs from the top of the candy to the
wax paper. Let the spider sit for a few hours to completely harden.
Then place your spider on the cookie's green puddle before it dries.

IN THE Doghouse

Warm your heart with this sweet treat. Pet lovers will adore this playful twist on a gingerbread house.

INGREDIENTS

edge royal icing
9 square graham crackers
blue food coloring
1 large marshmallow
1 small gingersnap cookie
flood royal icing
1 brown jelly bean
2 mini chocolate chips
1 chocolate chew
1 red round fruit candy
1 sour candy strip

1. Place most of the edge icing in a piping bag. Leave a small amount in a bowl. Pipe this white icing around the sides of one graham cracker. Place the cracker flat on a piece of wax paper.

2. Pipe around all four sides of the next graham cracker, and glue it upright to one side of the base. Repeat with the other three sides, gently squeezing them together.

3. Cut one of the graham cracker squares in half to form two triangles. Edge each with icing and place one on top of the front "wall" and one on the back wall.

4. Pipe around the last two crackers and place them on the triangles to make a roof.

5. Let the doghouse sit for 15 minutes. Then pipe edge icing on the roof to make icicles.

6. Tint the bowl of icing with blue food coloring. Put in a piping bag.

7. Cut the last cracker into fourths. Pipe your puppy's name on one of the cracker pieces. Glue the name tag to the roof with white icing. Set the house aside to harden for about an hour.

8. To make your puppy, cut the large marshmallow in half. Use edge icing to glue a marshmallow half onto the cookie as a snout.

9. Spoon white flood icing over the marshmallow and cookie. Stick on the jelly bean as a nose and the two chocolate chips for eyes.

10. Warm the chocolate chew in the microwave for five seconds. Place it between two pieces of wax paper and roll it flat with a rolling pin. Cut two ear shapes from the candy, and place them on the dog's head.

11. Place a red fruit candy on the side of the snout for a tongue.

12. Let your puppy harden for about an hour. Then glue him on the front of the doghouse with some edge frosting.

13. Cut the sour candy strip into a hat shape. Glue it onto the dog's head with a little icing. Trim the ends of the candy strip to look like a scarf. Tuck these under his neck with a little edge frosting.

Tip:
In this project, the icing in the piping bag will sit between uses. The icing may harden and clog up the tip. To prevent this, wet a paper towel and put it in the bottom of a glass. Place your piping bag in the glass so the tip sits on the wet towel.

BUGGING OUT

Buzz around the kitchen to make these bee-utiful bugs. Finally some bugs people want at their picnic!

INGREDIENTS
edge royal icing
red and yellow food coloring
flood royal icing
1 black licorice whip
2 chocolate sandwich cookies
flood icing
8 mini chocolate chips
2 chocolate sprinkles
2 pale yellow candy wafers

1. Divide the edge icing into three small bowls. Add red food coloring to one and yellow food coloring to another. Keep the third bowl white.

2. Divide the flood icing into two small bowls. Add red food coloring to one bowl and yellow to the other to match the edge icing.

3. Cut six small pieces of licorice whip for the legs. Open the top of one sandwich cookie. Pipe three dots of white edge icing along each side to hold the six legs. Squeeze a blob of icing in the middle of the cookie and glue the top back on.

4. With the red edge icing, pipe the shape of two red wings on top of the cookie. Spoon the red flood icing into the wing areas. Spread it with a toothpick to cover well.

5. While the icing is still wet, add six mini chocolate chips as spots. With the white edge icing, pipe two small eyes. Stick chocolate sprinkles in for eyeballs.

6. Cut a small piece of licorice whip for the bee's stinger. Open the top of the other sandwich cookie. Pipe a dot of white edge icing on the bottom and glue on the stinger.

7. Pipe lines of edge icing on each side of the inside of the cookie. Place one candy wafer on each side as wings. Squeeze a blob of icing in the middle of the cookie and glue the top back on.

8. Pipe three bands of yellow edge icing on top of the cookie. Spoon yellow flood icing into the bands and cover well.

9. While the icing is still wet, add two mini chocolate chips as eyes.

10. Let the cookies sit for a few hours to completely harden.

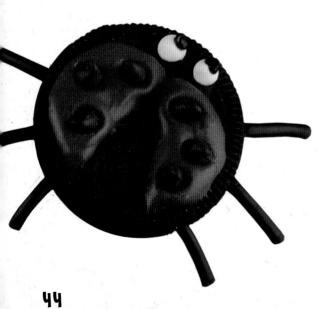

FAIRY RING

Legend says that rings of mushrooms grow where fairies danced. Coax the shy little sprites out of hiding for a magical party of your own.

INGREDIENTS

flood royal icing
red food coloring
brown food coloring
5 vanilla wafer cookies
3 oatmeal cookies
edge royal icing
5 large marshmallows
5 chocolate chews
pink, green, and yellow taffy

1. Divide the flood icing into two bowls. Add red food coloring to one. Tint the other bowl light brown.

2. Place the vanilla wafers on a cooling rack, with a piece of wax paper below them. Spoon red flood icing over each cookie so it completely covers them. Let them sit for about an hour.

3. Stack the oatmeal cookies together with a spoonful of brown flood icing between each later. Completely cover the top cookie with brown flood icing. Set aside to harden for about an hour.

4. Divide the edge icing into two small bowls. Make one bowl dark brown. Keep the other bowl white. Place the icing into piping bags.

5. With the white edge icing, pipe dots on the top of a red cookie. Then pipe a blob of icing on the bottom of it. Place the cookie on top of a marshmallow. Repeat with the other cookies and marshmallows.

6. Warm the chocolate chews between two pieces of wax paper in the microwave for about five seconds. Roll them flat with a rolling pin.

7. Mold the chews onto the outside of the cookie stack to look like bark.

8. With the brown edge icing, pipe circles on the stump to look like tree rings.

9. With the white edge icing, pipe fairy wings on a piece of wax paper. Set aside to harden for about two hours.

10. Warm the pink taffy in the microwave. Roll a small round ball for the head and longer pieces for arms, legs, and a body. Mold them together to look like a person.

11. Warm the green taffy and roll it flat. Cut out the shape of a dress. Wrap the dress around the pink body. Mold the bottom part to look like a wavy skirt.

12. When the wings have hardened, gently push them onto the back of the fairy.

13. Warm the yellow taffy and roll it flat. Cut it into thin strips. Wrap these strips around a toothpick to make them curly. Place them on the fairy's head as hair.

14. To display your fairy ring, place the stump in the center and perch your taffy fairy on top. Surround it with the mushrooms.

SPACEY TREATS

Look who landed at your party! These spaceship and alien cookie pops will transport you to a delicious dimension.

INGREDIENTS
2 vanilla wafer cookies
edge royal icing
green food coloring
flood royal icing
2 green jelly beans
2 large red gumdrops
1 chocolate striped
    shortbread cookie
sugar pearls

Tip:
To display your treats, cover a block of Styrofoam with colorful paper. Then poke your pops in the foam so they stand up.

---

1. Cut the bottom edges of the vanilla wafer cookies so they have a pointed tip.

2. Tint the edge icing green.

3. Scoop a generous blob of edge icing onto the tip of a lollipop stick. Place the stick with frosting on the flat side of one of the cookies. Top it with the other cookie like a sandwich. Let the "cookie pop" harden for about an hour.

4. Tint the flood icing green to match your edge icing.

5. Dip the cookie pop into the green flood icing. Twirl it back and forth and tap the stick on the side of the bowl so the extra frosting drips off.

6. Place the pop flat on a cooling rack with wax paper below to catch extra drips. While the icing is still wet, place on two jelly beans to look like eyes. Let it sit for an hour or more to harden.

7. Thread a gumdrop upside down on a lollipop stick. Next, place the striped cookie upside down. Finally, add another gumdrop on top to hold the cookie on.

8. Pipe green edge icing around the cookie's top edge. Use tweezers to place sugar pearls along the icing line to look like lights.

CURLED UP
COZY CAT

**Curl up with this cozy kitty cat treat.
And see how sweet your fortune can be!**

INGREDIENTS
edge royal icing
green and orange food coloring
1 large round sugar cookie
flood royal icing
1 fortune cookie
1 piece pink taffy
1 pink gum ball
2 chocolate sprinkles

1. Take a spoonful of the edge icing and color it green. Divide the rest of the edge icing into two bowls. Color one bowl orange. Leave the other bowl white. Put the icings in piping bags.

2. Pipe a circle of orange edge icing around the sugar cookie.

3. Tint the flood icing orange to match the edge icing.

4. Spoon orange flood icing into the center of the cookie. Use a toothpick to spread it out.

5. Place the fortune cookie on a cooling rack with wax paper beneath. Spoon orange flood icing over the fortune cookie until it is covered. Set both cookies aside to harden for about an hour.

6. Glue the fortune cookie head onto the cookie body with a small dab of icing.

7. Pipe white edge icing on the round cookie to look like a body and tail. Add stripes of white edge icing on the fortune cookie to make face stripes and ear tips.

8. Warm the pink taffy in the microwave for about 5 seconds. Place it in between two pieces of wax paper and roll it flat. Cut out a tiny triangle. With a dab of icing, glue it onto the cat's face as the nose.

9. Cut the rest of the taffy into long, thin strips. Roll them smooth. Wrap them around a gum ball. If you wish, glue the gum ball to the cookie so it looks like the cat has snuggled up with a ball of yarn.

10. With the green edge icing, pipe two small eyes on the fortune cookie. With tweezers, place a chocolate sprinkle vertically within each one.

11. Let the cookie sit for a few hours to completely harden.

FLOWER PLACE CARD

Flowers are a perfect accent for any table setting. Use these personalized place cards to make every guest feel special.

INGREDIENTS

4 large round sugar cookies
pink, green, and yellow
    food coloring
edge royal icing
flood royal icing
sugar pearls
5 chocolate melting wafers

1. Use a cookie cutter to cut a flower shape from one cookie. If the cookie isn't soft enough, place it in the microwave for about 10 seconds before cutting.

2. Use a cookie cutter to cut large leaves from two cookies.

3. Mix up batches of pink and green edge icing. Place the icings in piping bags.

> *Tip:*
> A party host often tries to make all the elements on the table match. Use colors on your place cards that match the napkins, plates, and flowers on your party table.

4. With the pink edge icing, pipe around the outer edge of the flower cookie. Also pipe around the inner edge of the petals, leaving an open area in the center.

5. With the green edge icing, pipe around the edges of the leaf cookies.

6. Mix up batches of pink, yellow, and green flood icing. Spoon the pink icing into the petals of the flower cookie. Spoon the yellow icing into the center of the flower. Spread the icing with a toothpick.

7. With a tweezers, place sugar pearls around the flower's center.

8. Spoon green flood icing on the leaves, using a toothpick to spread.

9. Let the cookies harden for an hour.

10. Place the melting wafers in a small zip-top bag. Leave the bag open and microwave on the defrost setting for 30 seconds. Squeeze the melted candy to one corner. If the wafers are not soft yet, microwave on defrost 30 seconds more. With a kitchen shears, snip off the corner of the bag.

11. Pipe the melted chocolate on the flower, spelling a friend's name.

12. Use edge icing to glue together the three pieces. The flower should be in the center, overlapping the leaves. Let harden for about 15 minutes.

13. Cut the last round cookie in half. Use edge icing to glue half of the cookie onto the back of the flower as a stand.

14. Let the cookies sit for a few hours to completely harden.

monkey AROUND

Sock monkeys are some of the most popular stuffed animals. Bring your toy to the table and have some fun playing with your food.

INGREDIENTS
edge royal icing
red food coloring
flood royal icing
oval cookie
1 black licorice whip
1 large round sugar cookie
decorating sugar, any color
1 red licorice whip
2 brown candy-coated
    chocolates
2 candy wafers

1. Divide the edge icing into two small bowls. Add red food coloring to one and leave the other bowl white. Place the icing into piping bags.

2. Divide the flood icing into two small bowls. Add red food coloring to one to match the edge icing. Keep one bowl white.

3. Pipe red edge icing in an oval shape on top of the oval cookie.

4. Spoon the white flood icing over the cookie, being careful not to get any inside the red oval. Then spoon red flood icing inside the oval. Use a toothpick to completely cover.

5. Cut a short length of black licorice whip and place it in the red area for a mouth. Let the cookie harden for 20 minutes.

6. With the white edge icing, pipe a half circle around just over half of the sugar cookie. Then pipe a stripe of frosting where the monkey's forehead would be. Leave an empty space between the half circle and the stripe, and a small space at the top.

7. Spoon white flood icing into the white areas.

8. While the icing is still wet, sprinkle decorating sugar on the white icing. Then put the mouth cookie on the sugar cookie.

9. Pipe stripes with the white edge icing above and below the sugared forehead stripe to fill in the empty areas.

10. Cut a few small strips of red licorice whip and place on top as hair. Place the two candy-coated chocolates as eyes.

11. With the white edge icing, pipe a semi circle on each of the candy wafers. Fill in with the white flood icing. Sprinkle with decorating sugar.

12. With the white edge icing, glue the wafers onto each side of the monkey's head as ears.

13. Let the cookie sit for a few hours to completely harden.

FRUIT SLICES

Enjoy a colorful slice of summer any time of year with cookies shaped like your favorite fruits.

INGREDIENTS
edge royal icing
flood royal icing
green, brown, orange, and pink
    food coloring
3 large round sugar cookies
chocolate sprinkles

1. Mix up a batch of edge icing. Divide into four bowls. Keep one bowl white, and tint the other bowls green, brown, and dark orange. Place the icings in piping bags.

2. Mix up a batch of flood icing. Divide into four bowls. Keep one bowl white, and tint the other bowls pink, green, and light orange.

3. To make a watermelon, pipe green edge icing around the outer edge of a cookie. Spoon the pink flood icing into the center. Spread it with a toothpick. Drop chocolate sprinkles in the pink area as seeds.

4. To make a kiwi, pipe brown edge icing around the outer edge of another cookie. Spoon the green flood icing into the center. Spread with a toothpick. While the green icing is still wet, place a dab of white flood icing in the middle of the cookie. With a toothpick, drag the white icing out from the center toward the outer edge several times. Add chocolate sprinkles to look like seeds.

5. To make an orange, pipe dark orange edge icing around the outer edge of the third cookie. Spoon light orange icing into the center. Spread with a toothpick. While the light orange icing is still wet, pipe white flood icing in a circle next to the dark orange edge icing. Also place a dab of white flood icing in the middle of the cookie. Use a toothpick to drag the white icing out from the center toward the outer edge. Then drag the white icing toward the center from the outer edge.

6. Let the icing harden for at least one hour. Then use a sharp knife to cut each cookie in half.

ROLLED-UP ROSES

Share the love with these edible flowers. Roses have never been this beautiful ... or sweet!

INGREDIENTS
6 packs of red fruit leather
1 pack green fruit leather

SPECIAL SUPPLIES
12 lollipop sticks

1. Cut the fruit leather into ¾-inch (2-centimeter) wide strips.

2. Cut 1-inch (2.5-cm) wide ovals from the strips. Each oval should have one straight edge. You'll need 16 "petals" for each rose.

3. Hold a lollipop stick in one hand. Roll one of the petals tightly around the top. Squeeze to mold the petal onto the stick.

4. Add the next petal, slightly overlapping the first. Squeeze the base with your fingers. Repeat with the remaining petals, moving around the flower as you go. Fold some of the petals out slightly at the top.

5. Cut two leaf shapes out of the green fruit leather. Place the wide edge of one leaf about 1 inch (2.5 cm) down from the base of your flower. Squeeze it onto the stick up to the flower's base. Repeat on the opposite side with the other leaf.

6. Repeat the steps to make additional flowers.

Tip:
If you'd like to give these as a gift, gather them together like a bouquet. Then tie a ribbon around the middle. Wrap the bunch in a cone of paper, just like they do at a flower shop.

WINTER ICICLES

Long sparkling icicles are like winter jewelry on buildings. Bring that bling indoors, and make your home a winter wonderland.

INGREDIENTS
10 white rock candy strings
10 light blue rock candy strings
10 dark blue rock candy strings

SPECIAL SUPPLIES
16-gauge turquoise
    aluminum wire
⅛-inch (.3-cm) wide
    blue ribbon
7½-inch (19-cm) wire wreath
    frame, spray painted silver

1. Cut the aluminum wire into 30 1½-inch (4-cm) long pieces.

2. Bend both ends of each wire piece around a pencil to form hook shapes.

3. Cut four pieces of ribbon 18 inches (46 cm) long. Tie these pieces to the wire wreath, evenly spaced around the circle. Tie the loose ends together in a tight knot.

4. Wrap additional ribbon around the wire wreath to add a decorative touch.

5. Hang the wreath where you want to display it.

6. Hang the wire hooks around the wreath on the outermost ring.

7. Hang one candy string on each wire hook, alternating colors as you go around the circle.

~ Finding the Fun ~
Some stores carry rock candy strings. But in some places, they might be hard to find. If you have trouble finding them, ask a parent to order the candy strings from online stores.

RISING STARS

Let your creativity twinkle with this star-studded project. Who knew hard candy could shine so brightly?

INGREDIENTS
10 hard fruit candies

SPECIAL SUPPLIES
hammer
star-shaped cookie cutter
clear thread (optional)

Tips:
Many types of hard candies will work for this project. But only use one kind at a time. The candies may have different melting points, so mixing them could cause problems for your project.

Some ovens run a bit hotter than others. Watch your candy through the oven window. You want the candies to melt completely. But don't let them heat up so much they bubble.

1. Preheat the oven to 350 degrees Fahrenheit (177 degrees Celsius).

2. Unwrap the candies and place in a sturdy zip-top bag. With a hammer, crush the candies into powdery bits. The finer the bits, the easier they will melt.

3. Line a cookie sheet with parchment paper. Pour the crushed candies onto the paper. Gently shake the tray so the crushed candies make a flat layer. Make sure you can't see the parchment paper between any of the candy bits.

4. Place the cookie sheet in the oven for three minutes.

5. Using an oven mitt, take the tray out of the oven. Let the candy cool for two minutes.

6. Working quickly, press the cookie cutter into the melted candy. Repeat until you've made as many stars as you can.

7. If you want to hang the stars later, grab a toothpick. Poke a hole in one point of each star.

8. Carefully move the parchment from the cookie sheet to a cooling rack. Let the pieces cool and harden completely.

9. Gently lift the hardened candy from the paper. Carefully break off the candy around each star.

10. If you want to make more stars, collect the scrap pieces, recrush them, and repeat steps 1–9.

11. To hang your stars, poke a piece of clear thread through the hole in each star and tie a knot.

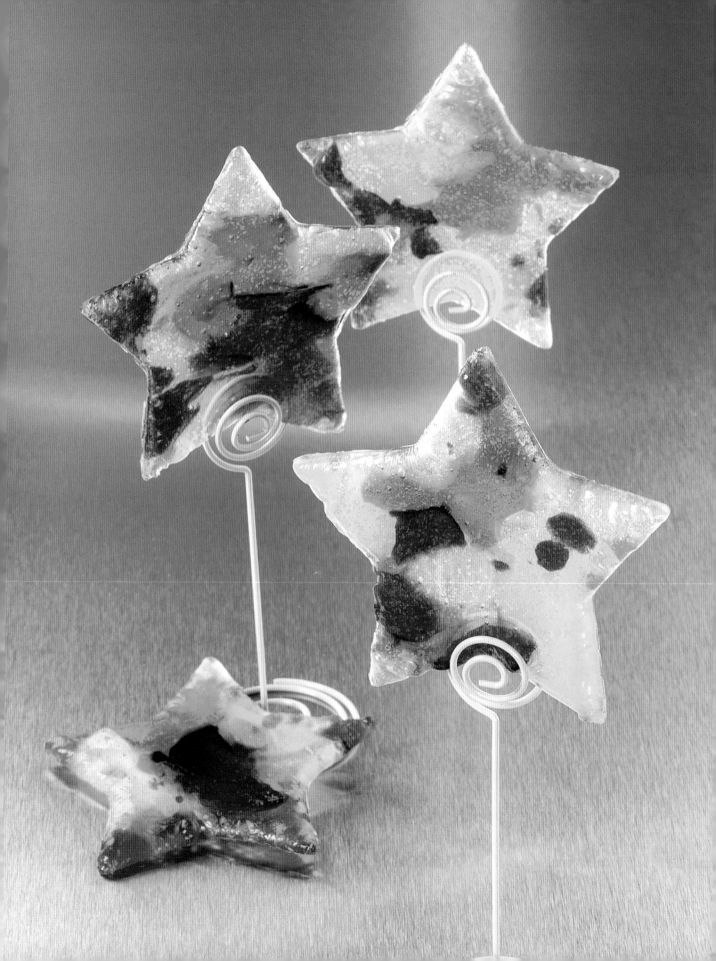

PICK·A·FLOWER PARTY FAVORS

Imagine a world where candy grows on trees. Then make it happen! Make a tree of sweet little blossom bundles that make perfect "goody bags" for your next party.

INGREDIENTS
600 small round candies

SPECIAL SUPPLIES
floral foam
small flower pot
silk flower stem
½-inch (1-cm) wide green
    grosgrain ribbon
12 9-inch (23-cm) white
    tulle circles
12 green twisty ties

1. With a knife, cut the piece of floral foam to fit into the flower pot. Poke the end of the stem into the foam.

2. Cut 12 pieces of ribbon 6 inches (15 cm) long.

3. Separate the candies by color.

4. Place 50 candies of the same or similar colors in the center of a tulle circle. Gather up the sides and twist. Tie a piece of ribbon tightly around the tulle to hold in the candies.

5. Repeat step 4 with the other tulle pieces and candies.

6. Attach each blossom to the flower stem with a green twisty tie.

Tip:
Instead of buying a fake stem for this project, you could use a real branch. If you use a real branch, try to find one that is clean and sturdy. A branch that has lots of extra little branches works nicely.

LICORICE TWIST BUTTERFLIES

Bug out your family and friends. This unusual use of licorice will have them fluttering with excitement.

INGREDIENTS
rainbow licorice twists

SPECIAL SUPPLIES
iron

1. Turn a cookie sheet upside down on your workspace. Cover it with a dish towel. Place a piece of parchment paper on top of the towel.

2. On a cutting board, cut the licorice twists into ¼-inch (.6-cm) slices with a knife to form star-shaped beads. You need two blue, six green, 14 purple, 16 red, and 18 yellow beads to make the butterfly. Or use whatever colors you want!

3. Arrange the beads on the piece of parchment in the shape of a butterfly. Start with a center line as its body. Then place the beads symmetrically on each side. Make sure the beads are all touching.

4. Put another piece of parchment paper on top of your butterfly. With a dry iron set on the cotton setting, press the iron down on the parchment. Hold it in place for 10 to 15 seconds. Lift the iron and set aside.

5. Carefully flip over the pieces of parchment with the butterfly inside. Press the iron on the other side of the parchment for 10 to 15 seconds.

6. Peel off the top piece of parchment. Let the bead butterfly cool completely.

~ *Endless Possibilities* ~
You can make any shape you want with this project. Just make sure every licorice bead touches at least one other bead before ironing. Then your project will be nice and sturdy.

CANDY SHAKE

Layer up the candy for this twist on a milkshake. This treat is so sweet, friends will want to take it home to eat. And they don't have to worry about it melting!

INGREDIENTS
pink, white, and brown candies
(Use any kinds you like!)
cotton candy
candy cane stick
1 red candy

1. In a clear glass, make a layer of pink candy.

2. Place a layer of white candy on top of the pink.

3. Sprinkle in some brown candies to look like hot fudge.

4. Make a small layer of white candy. Then add a small layer of pink.

5. Next add a layer of brown candies.

6. Place a bit of cotton candy on top to look like whipped cream.

7. Stick the candy cane into the candy shake. Then put a red candy on top like a cherry.

Tip:
These candy shakes make fun party place cards. Layer the candy in clear plastic cups. Write your guests' names on the outside of each cup with a permanent marker. Place one shake at each spot so they know where to sit. Then they can nibble on the treats for dessert.

mix·and·match
MONSTERS

Show off your scary side with these gummy monsters. With just a few candy details, create a whole crew of creatures with attitude.

INGREDIENTS
large sugared gumdrops
vanilla frosting

For the monster's features, use any small candies you like. Here are some ideas:

banana-shaped candies
candy buttons
licorice whips
rainbow licorice twists
rainbow sprinkles
round breath mints
round gummy candies
small breath mints
small gumdrops
sugar pearls
wafer candies

1. Use large gumdrops as the monsters' bodies. Use a toothpick to dig small holes in the gumdrops. Put holes wherever you want to add facial features.

2. Use different candies to make faces for your monsters. Put the candies into the holes you dug to make them stick.

3. Add hair, feet, or other features to your monsters. Use dabs of vanilla frosting to stick on large candies.

Be creative and have fun!

sweet sushi

Try this twist on sushi. And fool your family with dinner for dessert!

INGREDIENTS
1 large marshmallow
1 red and 1 green gumdrop
1 crispy rice marshmallow treat
2 packs green fruit leather
8 round cinnamon candies
1 piece each of pink, orange, and white taffy

1. Cut the marshmallow in half width wise with the kitchen shears. The cut ends will be sticky.

2. With a knife, cut off the round tops from both gumdrops. Then cut the tops in half lengthwise. Press one red piece and one green piece together. Repeat with the other red and green pieces

3. Cut off about ½ inch (1 cm) from one end of the crispy rice treat. Mold the cut piece in a circle around a red/green gumdrop. Make the circle the same size as the marshmallow half from step 1. Then place the crispy circle on the sticky end of one marshmallow half.

4. With the kitchen shears, cut a strip of fruit leather the same height as the marshmallow and crispy circle. Roll the fruit leather strip around the marshmallow and crispy circle. Press the end to seal.

5. Repeat steps 3 and 4. Then stick eight cinnamon candies on top of this piece to look like fish eggs.

6. Warm the pink, orange, and white taffy in the microwave for about five seconds. Place each one between two pieces of wax paper, and roll them flat with a rolling pin.

7. Mold the pink taffy into a long rectangle. Use a toothpick to draw evenly spaced lines across the top of the taffy to look like tuna.

8. Mold the orange taffy into a long rectangle. Then trim one end to look like a tail. Use a toothpick to draw lines on the top of this "shrimp."

9. With kitchen shears, cut thin strips out of the white taffy. Lay two strips across the pink taffy. Lay two strips slightly curved across the orange taffy. Press the strips down gently to lay flat.

10. With a knife, cut two 2-inch (5-cm) rectangles from the crispy rice treat. Place the tuna on one piece and the shrimp on the other.

11. Cut two thin strips of fruit leather. Wrap them around the tuna and shrimp and crispy rice rectangles.

EARTH BEAD BRACELET

Home sweet home. Celebrate our home planet with an Earth-inspired bracelet. Made with "candy clay," it shows off our sweet home indeed!

INGREDIENTS

2.5 ounces (71 grams) each
    of green and blue candy
    melting wafers
8 teaspoons (40 mL)
    light corn syrup

SPECIAL SUPPLIES

2–3 wooden skewers
3 12-inch (30-cm) long blue or
    green hemp beading cords

1. Place the green melting wafers in a microwave safe bowl and heat according to the package directions. When the wafers are fully melted, add 4 teaspoons of light corn syrup. Stir until smooth dough forms.

2. Place the dough on a piece of wax paper. Flatten with a spoon slightly so it is about ¼-inch (.6-cm) thick.

3. Repeat steps 1 and 2 with the blue melting wafers.

4. Set the doughs aside for 30 minutes to harden. They will become stiff like clay.

5. Pinch off a piece of blue dough and roll it into a ½-inch (1-cm) ball. Then pinch off three to five smaller pieces of green dough and stick them onto the blue ball. Roll the ball again so that all the dough is flat and smooth.

6. Repeat with the rest of the dough, rolling beads of blue and sticking on small pieces of green.

7. With a toothpick, poke a hole through each dough bead. Run the toothpick back and forth through the beads so that they can move freely. Reroll the beads gently if they get a little stretched when you push the toothpick through.

8. Thread the beads onto skewers, leaving a small space between each bead. Put the skewers on a cookie sheet.

9. Place the cookie sheet in the refrigerator for an hour. Check on the beads every 15 minutes to make sure they roll freely and aren't sticking to the skewer or to each other.

10. Remove the beads from the skewers.

11. Hold the beading cords together evenly across your workspace. Thread 12 beads onto the cords. Hold the bracelet around your wrist to check the size. Add or remove beads for the perfect fit.

12. Tie both ends of the beading cord together to secure.

FLOWER TURTLES

After a busy day, a turtle treat might help slow things down. But prepare yourself. These tasty turtles will move fast when friends get a taste!

INGREDIENTS
12 pieces sliced almonds
60 pieces slivered almonds
12 chocolate-covered caramels
1 sheet candy buttons

1. Preheat the oven to 350 degrees Fahrenheit (177 degrees Celsius).

2. Line a cookie sheet with parchment paper.

3. Place a sliced almond on the paper as the head. Place five slivered almonds in a star shape to make the legs and tail. Make sure the legs and tail all meet in a center point.

4. Place a chocolate-covered caramel on the center point of the almond star.

5. Repeat steps 3–4 with the rest of the almonds and chocolate-covered caramels.

6. Bake the turtles for about three to four minutes, enough to start melting the chocolate and caramel.

7. With an oven mitt, take the cookie sheet out of the oven. While the chocolate is still warm, place the candy buttons on top of the "shells" in a flower shape. Push the candy down gently. The chocolate will spread out a little.

8. When the cookie sheet is cool to the touch, place it in the refrigerator so the turtles can harden.

Tip:
You don't have to use almonds for this project. Look for other nuts or nut pieces shaped like heads, legs, and tails. Peanuts or cashews would work well too.

LOLLIPOP DISCO BALL

Get the party started with this glittery disco ball. But this decoration won't go to waste. It'll provide sweet treats for your guests when the dancing is done.

INGREDIENTS
250 to 300 small
    round lollipops

SPECIAL SUPPLIES
1 7-inch (18-cm) Styrofoam
    ball
plastic beaded necklace
250 to 300 4-inch (10-cm)
    squares of aluminum foil

~ Light It Up ~
You can make this disco ball into a light for your dance floor. Before you push in the lollipops, wrap the ball with a string of white lights. Tape the lights down in a few places. Then push in the pops to cover the cords, letting the lights stick out between them. The lights will reflect off the foil and really make your disco ball shine!

1. With a long wooden skewer, poke a hole through the center of the ball from top to bottom. Thread the plastic necklace through the hole. Use the wooden skewer to help push the necklace through.

2. Tie one end of the necklace in a knot. Make sure the knot is much bigger than the hole. The disco ball will get heavy, and you need to be sure the necklace won't slip out. Pull the necklace so the knot is even with the bottom of the disco ball and you have a loop for hanging at the top.

3. Place the top of a lollipop in the center of an aluminum foil square. Gather the corners of the foil around the base of the lollipop and twist to tighten the paper. Repeat on all of the lollipops.

4. Poke the lollipops into the ball in a horizontal line around the middle. Space the lollipops about 1 inch (2.5 cm) apart.

5. Add a second line just above the first, tucking each lollipop between the ones on the first line.

6. Continue adding lines of pops all the way up to the top.

7. Repeat on the lower half of the ball, adding rings of lollipops until you reach the knot on the bottom.

TREASURE chest

X marks the spot to a tasty treasure. Discover this sweet chest bursting with candy gold. You might not want to share this delicious booty!

INGREDIENTS
chocolate and yellow candy
   melting wafers
6 bars of crisp wafers in chocolate
   (Do not break the bars apart.)
4 banana-shaped candies
gold-wrapped chocolate candies
candy necklaces
candy-coated chocolates

1. Place the chocolate melting wafers in a small zip-top bag. Leave the bag open and microwave on the defrost setting for 30 seconds. Squeeze the melted candy to one corner. If the wafers are not soft yet, microwave on defrost 30 seconds more. With a kitchen shears, snip off the corner of the bag.

2. Place one bar of wafers on your work surface with the bottom facing up. This will be your base.

3. Lay another bar of wafers down with the bottom facing up. Pipe melted chocolate around the sides. Glue this bar to one side of the base. Repeat with the other three sides, gently squeezing the sides together.

4. Place a few yellow melting wafers in a zip-top bag. Melt them as you did in step 1.

5. Use the yellow melted candy to glue banana-shaped candies to the chest as handles. Pipe small dots on the front as decoration.

6. Fill the chest with candy treasures, such as gold-wrapped chocolate candies, candy necklaces, and candy-coated chocolates.

7. Pipe a line of melted chocolate along the top back edge of the chest. Place the last crisp wafer bar along this line. It will stay propped open by the candy treasure. Pipe small yellow dots on the top as decoration. Add a banana-shaped candy as a top handle.

COASTER CAKe

Do you crave the sweet thrill of a roller coaster? Create the ups and downs with this very tasty attraction.

INGREDIENTS

1 8-inch (20-centimeter)
    square cake
2 9-inch (23-cm) round cakes
vanilla frosting
green, blue, and brown
    food coloring
red licorice whips
rainbow licorice twists
gum balls
pretzel sticks
8 teddy bear crackers
4 fun-size candy bars
4 pieces each of red and yellow
    candy-coated chewing gum
16 round candy necklace pieces

1. Cut one round cake in half. Cut the other cake so one half is slightly larger than the other.

2. Lay the square cake on your cake board. Place the two evenly cut cake halves at each end of the square cake.

3. Mix up a batch of green frosting. Frost the cakes on the board.

4. Mix up a batch of blue frosting. Place the unevenly cut cake halves side-by-side on top of the green cake. Frost these two pieces blue.

5. Mix up a batch of brown frosting. Pipe horizontal tracks up and down the blue cakes and around the green cake.

6. Place the licorice whips on each side of the tracks. Use kitchen shears to cut whips to the lengths needed.

7. Use rainbow licorice twists to decorate around the sides of the green cake and the sides of the blue hills. Use kitchen shears to cut these to the right lengths too.

8. Use a dab of frosting to glue a gum ball to the top of each licorice twist.

9. Gently press pretzel sticks to the sides of the blue hills to look like supports for the roller coaster.

10. Pipe green frosting on the tops of the candy bars to look like seats.

11. With a sharp knife, cut the legs off the bear crackers. Pipe a line of frosting on the bottom edges of two bears. Glue them in their frosting "seats" on a candy bar. Repeat with the other bears and candy bars.

12. Use frosting to glue the candy-coated gum pieces on the front and back of each car for lights. Then glue four candy necklace pieces to each car as wheels.

13. Place the cars in a line on the cake, setting the wheels in the frosting tracks.

~ Cake Boards ~

You'll need something to put your cake creations on. Cut a piece of cardboard the same size or a little bigger than your cake. Lay the board on a piece of aluminum foil. Cut the foil larger than the board. Fold the foil over the back of the cardboard and tape flat.

FOOLED YOU
PB&J

A sandwich for dessert? You bet! Transform a favorite lunchtime food into an unexpected, and delicious, dessert.

INGREDIENTS
2 ½-inch- (1-cm-) thick
    slices of pound cake
peanut butter
vanilla frosting
raspberry jam
1 piece each of green and
    orange taffy

Tip:
Peanut butter and jelly aren't the only sandwich spreads you could create.
• White frosting looks like cream cheese.
• Tan frosting and white candy wafers edged with green frosting look like hummus and cucumber.
• Yellow frosting and red fruit leather look like grilled cheese with bacon.

Get creative, and make a whole deli of desserts!

1. With a knife, cut each pound cake slice in half width wise.

2. Mix 2 tablespoons (30 mL) peanut butter into the vanilla frosting. Use a clean spoon to taste the frosting. If you want a more peanutty taste, add more peanut butter in small amounts until it's just right.

3. Generously spread the peanut butter frosting on two halves of the "bread."

4. Spread jam on the other two halves.

5. Place the frosting and jam slices together.

6. For a pickle to put on the side, roll the green taffy between your hands to get a pickle shape. Then round the ends. Use a toothpick to poke small holes up and down the taffy.

7. To make carrots, flatten the taffy between sheets of wax paper with a rolling pin. Cut out strips that are about ½ inch (1 cm) wide. Gently press fork tines into the strip to make crinkles.

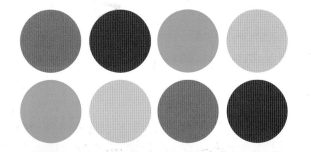

POOL PARTY

Nothing beats a relaxing day of poolside fun—except cake! Dive into this supersweet treat any time of year.

INGREDIENTS

blue gelatin
2 9x13-inch (23x33-cm)
    rectangular cakes
vanilla frosting
blue and yellow food coloring
blue and red taffy
1 stick chewing gum
yellow and red fruit leather
4 round breath mints

1. Make a batch of blue gelatin according to the package directions. Place it in the refrigerator. When it is halfway through its hardening time, take it out and stir it up with a spoon. Return to refrigerator to finish hardening.

2. Place one of the cakes on your cake board. Cut out a rectangle from the middle of the other cake. Set the removed rectangle of cake aside.

3. Spread frosting on top of the cake on the board. Place the cut cake on top. Mix up a batch of light blue frosting. Frost the top of the cake and the inside of the rectangle with blue frosting.

4. Mix up a batch of yellow frosting. Pipe the yellow frosting up the sides of the cake in wide, overlapping strips.

5. Spoon gelatin into the hole until it reaches the top to fill up your pool.

6. Warm the blue taffy in the microwave for about 5 seconds. Place it between two pieces of wax paper and roll it flat with a rolling pin. With kitchen shears, cut the flat taffy into 1-inch (2.5-cm) squares. Keep rolling and cutting taffy into squares until you have about 62 of them. Place them all around your pool, like tiles on a pool deck.

7. Pipe a wide line of yellow frosting around the edge of the pool.

8. To make a diving board, stack two pieces of red taffy at the edge of the pool. Glue on a stick of gum with a bit of frosting.

9. Cut a triangle from the removed center piece of cake. Cover with blue frosting. With a kitchen shears, cut a strip of yellow fruit leather to lay over the triangle for a slide. Press two round mints to the sides to look like railings. Place the slide near one corner of the pool.

10. Flatten pieces of red and blue taffy. Roll each into long, thin ropes. Then wrap the red rope around the blue rope. Put a short length of the rope on the pool deck. Use longer taffy ropes to decorate the outer edge of the cake.

11. Cut small strips of red fruit leather. Wrap the strips around the mints for life rings. Place on the pool deck.

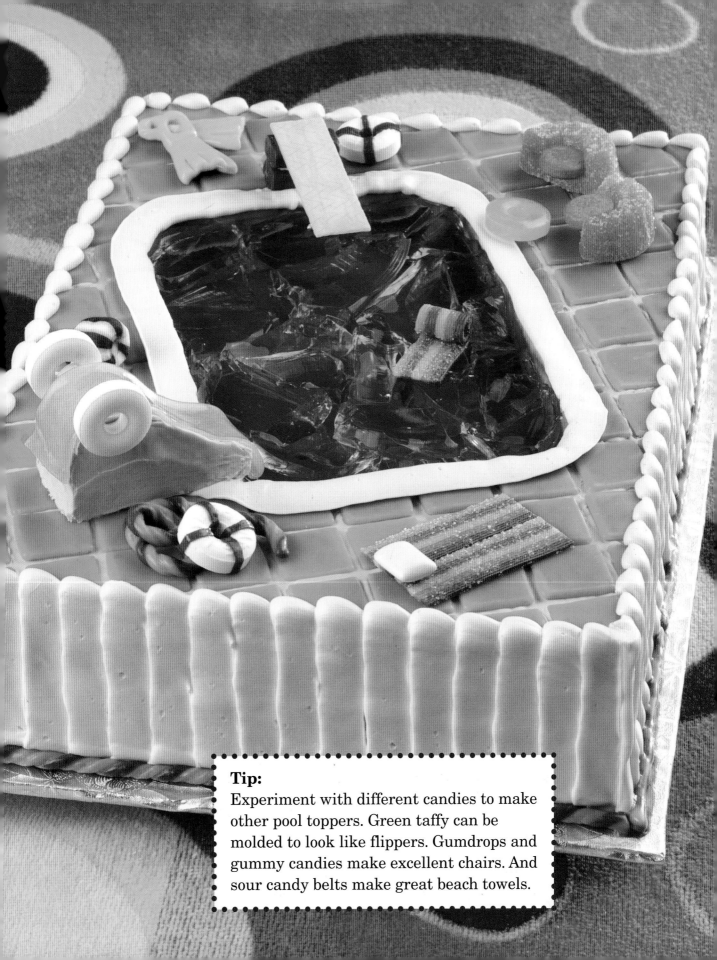

Tip:
Experiment with different candies to make other pool toppers. Green taffy can be molded to look like flippers. Gumdrops and gummy candies make excellent chairs. And sour candy belts make great beach towels.

BOX OF CHOCOLATES

Is it a box of chocolates? Is it a cake? It's both! Give two treats in one with this cake your friends will love.

INGREDIENTS

2 8-inch (20-cm) square cakes
vanilla frosting
pink, purple, green, and brown
    food coloring
a box of chocolates
    with about 16 pieces

Tips:
• For parts that need to be sturdy, professionals frost cake boards and Styrofoam instead of cake. Just be sure to warn your guests not to eat it!

• Level cakes so they'll lay flat when you stack them. With the cake at eye level, place your knife at the edge and skim it through the top of the cake. This cut will take off the higher middle part.

1. Level your cakes so the tops are flat. Place one cake on the cake board

2. Mix up a batch of pink frosting and frost the top of the cake on the board.

3. Cut a square out of the middle of the second cake, leaving just a 2-inch (5-cm) frame. Place the frame of cake on top of the frosted cake.

4. Cut an 8-inch (20-cm) square of cardboard. Cover it with aluminum foil and tape the foil to the back. This will be the "lid" of your box.

5. Frost the entire cake with pink frosting, including the inside of the hole. Also frost the top and edges of the cardboard square.

6. Open your real box of chocolates. Place the chocolates inside the hole of the cake.

7. Mix up batches of purple, green, and brown frosting. Pipe accents on the box and lid. Write a message on the lid. Be creative and have fun.

8. Gently set your lid at an angle against the cake to look like someone snuck into your box of chocolates.

TIE-DYE T-SHIRT

Get groovy with this retro cake. Set a food fashion trend with this tie-dye creation!

INGREDIENTS
1 9x13-inch (23x33 cm)
    rectangular cake
1 8-inch (20-cm) square cake
vanilla frosting
rainbow sprinkles
edge royal icing
flood royal icing
red, blue, yellow, and green
    food coloring

1. Trim out a half circle from one short end of the rectangular cake. This is the shirt collar.

2. Cut two sleeve shapes out of the square cake. Glue the sleeve pieces to the larger cake with some frosting.

3. Level the cakes so the top is completely flat.

4. Frost the top and sides of the cake with vanilla frosting. Press rainbow sprinkles onto the sides all around the cake.

5. Place the cake in the refrigerator for 30 minutes to firm up the frosting.

6. Meanwhile, mix up a batch of white edge icing and put in a piping bag.

7. Divide the flood icing into five bowls. Tint four of the bowls red, yellow, green, and blue. Leave one bowl white. Put each color in a separate piping bag.

8. Pipe white edge icing around the top edges of the cake. Then spoon white flood icing onto the cake. Spread icing with the back of the spoon to cover the top.

9. Starting in the middle of the cake, pipe a swirl of red flood icing. Continue the swirl to the outer edge of the cake. Don't forget to do the sleeves.

10. Pipe a yellow swirl next to the red swirl, leaving some white space between them.

11. Pipe a green swirl next to the yellow swirl. Then do a blue swirl.

12. While the flood icing is still wet, pull a toothpick through the icings. Pull the toothpick in a curved line from the center to the outside edge. Continue all around the cake to create a tie-dye effect.

13. Let the cake sit for a few hours to let the frosting harden.

ROCKIN' GUITAR

Plug into this sweet treat and get ready for a rocking good time. This electric guitar will pump up the volume of fun at your next party.

INGREDIENTS
2 9-inch (23-cm) round cakes
pink, orange, and yellow
    food coloring
vanilla frosting
edge royal icing
flood royal icing
1 dark chocolate bar,
    broken in pieces
3 long chocolate wafer candies
12 sugar pearls
3 round chocolate-covered mints
1 round brown candy-coated chocolate
chocolate melting wafers

1. Make a template of the shapes needed to make a guitar. Use them to cut shapes out of the cakes. Glue the pieces together with a little frosting on your board.

2. Level the top of the cake.

3. Mix up a batch of pink frosting. Spread over the top and sides of the cake. Pipe beads of frosting around the bottom edge. Place the cake in the refrigerator until the frosting gets firm, about 30 minutes.

4. Mix up a batch of edge royal icing. Color it pink to match your frosting.

5. Mix up a batch of flood royal icing. Divide into three bowls. Color one bowl orange, one yellow, and one pink.

6. With the pink edge icing, pipe a line around the top edge of the entire cake.

7. Spoon the pink flood icing onto the cake top to completely cover the cake.

8. While the pink flood icing is still wet, pipe yellow and orange flame shapes on the body of the guitar.

9. Let the icing harden for an hour.

10. When the icing has hardened slightly, but not completely set, place on the candy details. Place six chocolate bar pieces on the neck of the guitar.

11. Place two long chocolate candies in the middle of the body. Place another long chocolate candy at the top of the neck.

12. Align six sugar pearls along the bottom edge of the last long chocolate candy on the body. Put six pearls along the left edge of the top of the guitar.

13. Place three chocolate-covered mints and one candy-coated chocolate along the right side of the body.

14. Place a few melting wafers in a small zip-top bag. Leave the bag open and microwave on the defrost setting for 30 seconds. Squeeze the melted candy to one corner. If the wafers are not soft yet, microwave on defrost 30 seconds more. Then snip a small corner off the bag.

15. On a piece of wax paper, pipe six strings of chocolate, long enough to go from the top of the neck to the body. Let them harden for an hour. Then place them on the cake.

Tip:
Use templates to make cakes of any shape.
1. Sketch out your cake design on paper.
2. On another paper, trace the bottoms of the cake pans and cut out these shapes. Arrange the pan shapes over your sketch. Figure out how the pan shapes could be cut to make the shapes in the sketch. Then cut the pan circles into those shapes.
3. Place the cut paper shapes on the cakes. Cut the cakes along the papers' edges.
4. Put your cake together like a puzzle.

mini mice

Tiny mice have snuck into the kitchen to snatch some cheese. Create these cake critters for your next party, and guests will snatch them up.

INGREDIENTS
1 10.75-ounce (305-gram) frozen
   pound cake
chocolate frosting
5 chocolate kisses
10 sliced almonds
5 cherry stems
yellow and red food coloring
vanilla frosting
edge royal icing

1. With a melon baller, scoop out five balls from the cake.

2. Put the chocolate frosting in a microwave-safe bowl. Heat for about 15 seconds in the microwave. Stir. You want the frosting to be a liquid, pourable consistency. Heat another 15 seconds if it is still too thick.

3. Prepare your work surface by placing a piece of wax paper under a cooling rack.

4. Stick a ball of cake on a fondue fork. Swirl the ball in the chocolate frosting until it is well covered. Tap the fork onto the side of the bowl so the excess frosting drips off.

5. With a butter knife, push the ball off the fork onto the cooling rack. The extra frosting will drip down onto the wax paper.

6. While the icing is still wet, stick a chocolate kiss to the ball as a head. Poke two sliced almonds on top as ears. Stick a cherry stem to the back as a tail.

7. Repeat steps 4–6 with the rest of the cake balls. Let the mice sit for a few hours until the icing hardens.

8. Cut a wedge out of the leftover pound cake. With the melon baller, scoop out holes from the wedge's surface.

9. Mix up a batch of yellow frosting. Heat it in the microwave as in step 2.

10. Dip the wedge into the yellow frosting as in step 4, and transfer to the cooling rack. Let harden.

11. Pipe small dots of white frosting on the mice as eyes. Pipe chocolate frosting on as eyebrows.

12. Mix up a batch of red edge royal icing. Put it in a piping bag. Pipe a small red nose at the tip of each chocolate kiss.

These little bites of cake are called petit fours. Petit four is French for "small oven."

enchanting PEACOCK

Peacocks are elegant and stylish birds. They are also a surprising cake creation. Make this cake to reflect your glamorous, enchanting, and unique personality.

INGREDIENTS

edge royal icing
blue, orange, yellow, green, and black food coloring
35–40 oval-shaped cookies
4 tablespoons (60 mL) butter (plus some extra)
1 bag mini marshmallows
6 cups (1,440 mL) crispy rice cereal
3 9-inch (23-cm) round cakes
vanilla frosting
1 white candy wafer

1. Make a batch of edge icing and divide into five bowls. Tint the icing in each bowl so you have dark blue, light blue, orange, yellow, and green.

2. Pipe a dark blue heart shape on one end of each cookie. Let icing set until hard.

3. Next pipe a blue circle around the heart. Then pipe a large orange oval around the blue.

4. Pipe a yellow edge around the orange icing. Finally end with green around the cookie's edge. Feel free to get creative with the design of your cookies. When you're done let the cookies sit for a few hours.

5. Lay out a piece of wax paper. On the paper, pipe the icings into the shape of a peacock's crest of head feathers. Let it sit on the wax paper for a few hours.

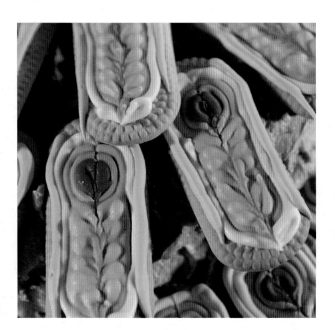

CONTINUED ON NEXT PAGE

6. With an adult's help, melt 4 tablespoons (60 mL) butter on medium heat in a large pot. Add the bag of marshmallows. Stir until they melt. Remove the pot from the heat, and pour in the cereal. Mix well.

7. Cover your workspace with a piece of wax paper. Coat it with some butter. Empty the pot of marshmallow treats onto the paper. Let it cool slightly. Rub butter all over your hands. Then mold the cereal into a head and neck shape.

8. Place the head into the refrigerator to harden for about 30 minutes.

9. Make a template of your three round cakes. Using the head as a guide, draw arches of cake to fit against the head in three steps. The bottom layer should be the biggest layer and the top the smallest. Use the templates to cut your cakes.

10. Place the crispy rice head on the cake board. Then place the bottom cake pieces against the head. Place the middle cake on top of that. Finally add the third layer. Trim the cakes as needed to make them fit against the head without too many gaps between.

11. Mix up a batch of blue frosting. Frost the head and body. On the head and neck, make small upward strokes with the spreader to make the frosting look like feathers.

12. Press cookies into the outside edge of the bottom cake. Space them as evenly as possible.

13. Add a second layer of cookies on top of the bottom cake. Offset the cookies a bit so they aren't directly above the cookies on the first layer.

14. Add three more layers of cookies, covering your peacock with feathers.

15. Arrange the icing crest on top of the peacock's head.

16. Mix a small batch of black frosting. Pipe a small eye on each side of the peacock's head.

17. Score the candy wafer with a knife. Then snap it in half along the line. Place one half on each side of the peacock's head just under the eye.

18. Use black and white frosting to add details to the eyes and nose.

MANI–PEDI DRESSER

Get the girls together for a spa night! Do your nails, braid your hair, and eat cake. What could be better than that?

INGREDIENTS
1 cake ball
1 black licorice twist, cut in half
pink, blue, and chocolate
    melting wafers
2 pieces hard stick candy
2 8-inch (20-cm) square cakes
chocolate frosting
vanilla frosting
1 chocolate bar
about 20 pink round candies

1. Make a cake ball from the recipe on the next page. Mold a spoonful of cake ball dough around one half of a licorice twist to make a nail polish bottle. Freeze the bottle for about an hour.

2. Melt the pink melting wafers according to package directions. Holding the licorice stem, dip the bottle into the melted candy. Set on wax paper to harden.

3. Draw a simple picture of a hand mirror on a piece of paper. Place a piece of wax paper over it.

4. Place a few blue melting wafers in a small zip-top bag. Leave the bag open and microwave on the defrost setting for 30 seconds. Squeeze the melted candy to one corner. If the wafers are not soft yet, microwave on defrost 30 seconds more. Then snip off a small corner of the bag.

5. Trace over your mirror drawing with the melted candy on the wax paper. If you wish, drizzle white or chocolate melted candy on the blue to create a design. Let the mirror harden.

6. Dip one side of a hard candy stick into the melted pink candy. Dip the second stick in the melted blue candy. Set both on wax paper to harden.

7. Level your cakes. Then glue the two layers together with frosting. Frost the entire cake with chocolate frosting.

8. Pipe vanilla frosting on the top to look like a lacy doily.

9. Break the chocolate bar along its ridges to create two rectangles. Glue them to the cake front with a dab of frosting. Pipe a small blob of vanilla frosting in the center of each rectangle to make drawers.

10. Place the bottle, mirror, and nail files on top of the cake.

11. Arrange the pink round candies on the cake to look like a necklace.

Cake balls are easy to make and tasty to eat.

Ingredients
One rectangular cake or two rounds.
One tub of frosting

Crumble the cake into a bowl so there are no large pieces.
Then add one spoonful of frosting at a time. Mix well after each
addition. Your mixture should be a moist dough that you can
mold into balls. If it seems too dry and falls apart easily, add
more frosting. You'll probably use most of a tub of frosting.

ZEBRA·STRIPED PURSE

Animal prints may reveal your wild side. But with so much frosting, you can't help being sweet too!

INGREDIENTS

2 8-inch (20-cm) square cakes
vanilla frosting
black and pink food coloring
2 red licorice twists
4 round breath mints
1 mini chocolate bar

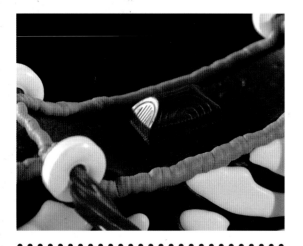

Tip:
Want to make a different shaped purse? Here are some ideas.
Clutch: Cut the cake in half to make a cordless clutch.
Satchel: Use two-thirds of the cake to make a satchel with small handles.

1. Glue the flat sides of the two cakes together with a layer of frosting. On each corner, poke a straw all the way through both layers. Trim off the extra straw that sticks out. These straws will help keep the layers together.

2. Cut a small semi-circle from one side of the cake, keeping the corners intact. This will be the top of the purse. Spread a little frosting on the opposite end, then stand the cake up on the cake board.

3. Mix up a batch of black frosting. Use it to frost all the sides of the cake.

4. Pipe outlines of white stripes across the sides of the cake. Then pipe more white frosting inside the outlines. Smooth out with a spreader.

5. Mix up a batch of pink icing. Pipe the pink frosting along the edges and base of the purse.

6. Thread each licorice twist through the holes of two mints. Carefully stick the mints on the purse to make handles.

7. Place the chocolate bar on top of the purse to make a clasp.

SUNFLOWER STICKS

Sunflowers make you think of warm summer days. Bring a little sunshine inside with these crafty cake pops.

INGREDIENTS
cake ball dough
yellow and chocolate candy
    melting wafers
15 candy corn pieces
chocolate sprinkles

1. Roll a spoonful of cake ball dough into a 1½-inch (4-cm) ball. Place on a cookie sheet lined with wax paper. Flatten the ball slightly into a thick disc shape.

2. Place a few yellow melting wafers in a small microwavable bowl. Melt according to package directions.

3. Roll the sides of the cake ball in the yellow melting candy.

4. While the candy is still wet, press candy corn into the ball to look like petals.

5. Let the flower dry for about an hour.

6. Place a few chocolate melting wafers in a zip-top bag. Leave the bag open and microwave on the defrost setting for 30 seconds. Squeeze the melted candy to one corner. If the wafers are not soft yet, microwave on defrost 30 seconds more. Then snip a small corner out of the bag.

7. Pipe the melted chocolate in a circle onto the face of the flower.

8. While the chocolate is still wet, drop on the chocolate sprinkles.

9. Let the pop dry for about an hour.

10. Poke a green straw into the cake ball behind the candy petals.

POLKA·DOT PRESENTS

Bring an unexpected present to the party. Pile on these cake presents, and unwrap a room full of smiles.

INGREDIENTS

6 8-inch (20-cm) square cakes
vanilla frosting
blue, orange, and green
    food coloring
36 sour candy strips
wafer candies
polka dot candies

1. Make cake boards for the layered cakes. Cut an 8-inch (20-cm) square, a 6-inch (15-cm) square, and a 4-inch (10-cm) square from cardboard. Cover each square with aluminum foil.

2. Level your cakes. Glue two cakes together with frosting. Repeat with the other cakes so you have three two-layer cakes.

3. Place one layered cake on the 8-inch (20-cm) board.

4. Cut one layered cake into a 6-inch (15-cm) square. Place it on the cake board of the same size.

5. Cut the last layered cake into a 4-inch (10-cm) square. Place it on the cake board of the same size.

6. Mix up batches of frosting in blue, orange, and green. Frost each cake with a different color.

7. Lay two sour candy strips over each side of the largest cake. Fold them up and over the edges to look like ribbon.

8. Place four plastic drinking straws into the top of the largest cake. Put them in a square shape near the middle. These will be supports for the second cake. With a kitchen shears, trim the straws level with the top of the cake.

9. Place the 6-inch (15-cm) cake with its cake board on top of the larger cake. Add sour candy strips and straw supports as in steps 7 and 8.

10. Stack the smallest cake on top. Add sour candy strips up the sides.

11. Loop the rest of the strips on top to look like a bow. Add wafer candies and polka dot candies all over the cakes.

sunny DAY CAKe

Heat up your next gathering with this "hot" dessert. This cake is so bright it's gotta wear shades!

INGREDIENTS
aqua and yellow food coloring
flood royal icing
2 round chocolate wafer cookies
vanilla frosting
1 9-inch (23-cm) round cake
24 orange fruit slices
about 24 yellow or orange
   candy-coated fruit candies
red licorice whip

1. Mix up a batch of aqua flood icing.

2. Lay the chocolate cookies side-by-side on a piece of wax paper, leaving a small space between them. Pipe flood icing onto the wax paper around the cookies to make sunglasses. Let the icing harden for at least one hour.

3. Mix up a batch of yellow frosting. Cover the cake with the yellow frosting.

4. Place the cookie sunglasses on the cake.

5. With kitchen shears, cut a length of licorice whip, and place it on the cake to make a smile. Cut two smaller pieces to put on the ends of the mouth.

6. Arrange the orange candy slices around the edge of the cake. Add fruit candies in between the slices.

DESERT DESSERT

Go wild—Wild West! But forget the campfire. With this creation you'll be singing songs around the cake!

INGREDIENTS
green, yellow, red, and chocolate
   candy melting wafers
3 oval-shaped cookies
4 vanilla wafer cookies
white sprinkles
1 potato chip
1 large gumdrop
1 piece blue taffy
4 peach ring candies
4 round candy necklace pieces
1 red sprinkle
brown food coloring
vanilla frosting
2 8-inch (20-cm) round cakes
8 graham crackers
candy rocks
3 chocolate chews

1. Place green melting wafers into a deep bowl. Melt according to package directions. Dip the oval-shaped cookies and the vanilla wafers into the melted candy. Place the dipped cookies onto wax paper. Place the vanilla wafers by the oval cookies so they will stick together and look like cacti. While the cookies are still wet, place white sprinkles on the cacti to look like spikes. Let them dry.

2. Scoop the rest of the green melting candy into a zip-top bag. Squeeze it all to one corner. Then snip off the corner.

3. Pipe the green melting candy onto the wax paper in cacti shapes. Make about 10 cacti. Sprinkle the cacti with white sprinkles while they are still soft. Let the candy harden for about 20 minutes.

4. Place a few yellow melting wafers in a zip-top bag. Leave the bag open and microwave on the defrost setting for 30 seconds. Squeeze the melted candy to one corner. If the wafers are not soft yet, microwave on defrost 30 seconds more. Then snip a small corner out of the bag. Repeat with the red wafers.

5. Pipe yellow flower shapes on the wax paper. Decorate the flowers with red accents. Let harden.

6. Pipe red melting wafers onto the wax paper into two flame shapes. Let harden.

CONTINUED ON NEXT PAGE

7. Melt chocolate melting wafers in a bowl according to package directions. Place a potato chip into the bowl, and spoon melted candy over it until it is well covered. Place it on a cooling rack, with a piece of wax paper below to catch the drips.

8. Cut a V-shaped groove in the top of a large gumdrop. Dip the gumdrop in the chocolate until well covered. Place it on top of the potato chip. Let harden.

9. Flatten a piece of blue taffy and roll into a thin rope. Place it around the hat.

10. Make a cut into three peach rings. Put the sticky ends together so they form a coil shape. Use a little frosting to glue four candy necklace pieces on one end like a rattle. Cut the last peach ring in half. Stick half onto the head end, turned the opposite way. With a toothpick, dab on melted chocolate dots as eyes. Poke a red sprinkle in the tip as a tongue.

11. Mix up a batch of brown frosting. Level your cakes, place on the cake board, and glue the two layers together with some frosting. Frost the entire cake.

12. Place the graham crackers into a zip-top bag. Crush the crackers into crumbs. Then sprinkle this "sand" over the top of the cake.

13. Push the cacti cookies into the top of the cake. For the campfire, make a ring of candy rocks. Place chocolate chew logs and candy flames in the center. Place the cowboy hat and snake on the cake too.

14. Press the candy cacti on the sides of the cake. Ring the bottom with candy rocks.